What to Do in an Emergency

by Christine Wolf

Editorial Offices: Glenview, Illinois • Parsippany, New Jersey • New York, New York
Sales Offices: Needham, Massachusetts • Duluth, Georgia • Glenview, Illinois
Coppell, Texas • Ontario, California • Mesa, Arizona

ISBN: 0-328-13248-9

8 9 10 V010 14 13 12 11 10 09 08

Emergencies don't happen very often. But when they do, kids can help. You can take care of yourself and your family. Sometimes you can help others too.

Be Prepared

What would you do if you were lost? What if you were in a fire or an accident? This book will tell you how to plan ahead.

Here are some things you can do now to be ready for an emergency:

- Learn how to call 9-1-1 for help.
- Know your address and phone number.
- Make an emergency plan with your family.
- Know where there is a first-aid kit in your home.

This boy knows how to call 9-1-1 for emergency help.

Getting Lost

Have you ever been lost? Know what to do when you are lost. That will help you stay calm. Here are some things to remember if it happens to you.

If You Are Indoors

- Go to the nearest counter or desk. Tell an adult you are lost.
- Know your address and phone number.

If You Are Outdoors

- Stay in the same spot.
- Listen for people calling your name.

Always stay close to the group if you are hiking outdoors.

Getting Out of a Fire

If you are in a house that is on fire, get out as fast as you can.

- Get down low. Smoke rises, so the air is easier to breathe closer to the floor.

- If your clothes are on fire, **stop**, **drop** to the ground, and **roll** to put the flames out.

- Break a window if it is the only way out.

- Don't stop to take anything with you.

Fire spreads quickly. Get to safety right away!

Once you are out of danger, you can call 9-1-1.

Don't try to rescue a person or pet in a fire. That is the job of the firefighters.

Let the firefighters fight the fire.

Getting Help in an Accident

What if you see an accident, such as a car crash? The first thing to do is to call 9-1-1.

Tell the operator what you saw. Speak clearly, so you can be heard. Don't hang up until the operator tells you to.

Do not try to move people who are hurt. The rescue team can do that. It is their job to pull people out of danger.

What if *you* are in the accident? Here are some tips:

- Stay calm and alert.
- Get out of danger.
- Check yourself for injuries.
- Call 9-1-1.

Remember: planning ahead can keep you safe!

Help prevent emergencies.
Always fasten your seatbelt.